HTML & CSS Made Simple

: Your Beginner's Handbook to Creating Modern, Responsive,
Interactive, and User-Friendly Websites

Matthew D.Passmore

Table of Contents

Introduction

The internet is an ever-expanding universe of information and connection. Every website you visit, from the corner bakery's menu to the latest news platform, is built with code. This code might seem like a complex mystery, but fear not! This book is your guide to unlocking the secrets of web development, starting with the foundational building blocks: HTML and CSS.

What exactly are HTML and CSS?*

Imagine a website as a house. HTML provides the framework, the walls, and the roof. It defines the structure of the content, like headings, paragraphs, images, and links. Think of it as the blueprint that tells the web browser where to place everything.

CSS, on the other hand, is the interior designer. It takes that bare structure and adds all the style – the paint colors, the furniture placement, the overall look and feel. CSS allows you to control the fonts, colors, layouts, and other visual elements that make your website visually appealing and user-friendly.

Why should you embark on this journey of learning HTML and CSS?*

The reasons are plentiful! Here are just a few:

Become a Website Architect: Ever dreamt of creating your own website? With HTML and CSS, you can turn your vision into reality, building a platform to showcase your hobbies, business, or simply something fun and creative.

Peek Behind the Curtain: Learning these fundamental languages gives you a deeper understanding of how websites function. No more black box! You'll be able to appreciate the intricate details that go into building the online world you navigate every day.

Unlock a World of Possibilities: HTML and CSS are the cornerstones of web development. Mastering them opens the door to further exploration. You can delve into the world of JavaScript to add interactivity, or explore frameworks that streamline complex web development processes.

Boost Your Career Prospects: Web development skills are highly sought after in today's job market. Having HTML and CSS in your toolbox makes you a valuable asset, opening doors to exciting career opportunities.

This book is your roadmap to mastering these foundational languages. Get ready to unleash your creativity and build a presence on the web!

1.1 What is HTML & CSS?

The internet is brimming with websites, each one a carefully crafted tapestry of information and design. But have you ever wondered what lies beneath the surface, creating the structure and visual appeal you experience? The answer lies in two fundamental languages: HTML and CSS.

HTML: The Blueprint of a Webpage

Imagine a website as a house under construction. HTML (HyperText Markup Language) acts like the blueprint, defining the basic structure and layout. It uses a series of tags, like labels, to tell the web browser how to organize the content. Headings, paragraphs, images, and links – all these elements are identified and positioned using HTML tags.

CSS: The Interior Designer of the Web

Once the structural framework is in place, it's time to add some flair! CSS (Cascading Style Sheets) takes on the role of the interior designer. It allows you to control the visual presentation of your webpage, like choosing the paint colors, furniture styles, and overall ambiance. With CSS, you can define the fonts, colors, backgrounds, layouts, and more, transforming the basic structure into a visually appealing and user-friendly experience.

In essence, HTML provides the foundation, the content and its organization, while CSS breathes life into it with style and design.

They work together seamlessly to create the websites we interact with every day.

1.2 Why Learn HTML & CSS?

The internet is like a vast digital landscape, and websites are the buildings that populate it. But unlike physical structures, these online creations require code to function. Learning HTML and CSS equips you with the essential tools to not just navigate this landscape, but to build your own structures within it. Here's why embarking on this journey is a wise decision:

Become a Web Architect: Ever dreamt of having your own online space? With HTML and CSS, you can transform your vision into reality. Build a website to showcase your passions, promote your business, or create a platform for creative expression. The possibilities are endless!

Unveil the Magic Behind the Web: Websites might seem like magic, but they're actually intricate puzzles built with code. By learning HTML and CSS, you'll gain a deeper understanding of how websites function. No more black box! You'll appreciate the thought and effort that goes into crafting the online experiences you use every day.

Unlock a Treasure Trove of Opportunities: HTML and CSS are the foundation of web development. Mastering them opens doors to a world of possibilities. You can delve into JavaScript to add dynamic interactivity, explore frameworks that streamline complex web development processes, or even build a career in the ever-growing field of web development.

Boost Your Career Prospects: Web development skills are highly sought after by businesses of all sizes. Having HTML and CSS in your toolbox makes you a valuable asset. These fundamental languages can open doors to exciting opportunities in web design, development, or even content management.

Learning HTML and CSS isn't just about code; it's about empowering yourself to create and participate in the digital world. It's a gateway to expressing yourself creatively, solving problems, and building something truly remarkable. So, are you ready to unleash your inner web architect?

Chapter 1
Getting Started with HTML

Welcome to the exciting world of HTML! This chapter will equip you with the basic building blocks to start crafting your own webpages. HTML, or HyperText Markup Language, is the foundation of any website, providing the structure and organization for the content you see. Think of it as the skeleton of a building, defining the framework for everything else to come.

Setting Up Your Development Environment:
Before we dive into code, let's prepare our workspace. You won't need any fancy software – a simple text editor will do the trick. Popular options include Notepad (Windows) or TextEdit (Mac). These programs allow you to write plain text, which is perfect for crafting HTML code.

The Basic Structure of an HTML Document:
Every HTML document follows a specific format. It starts with a <!DOCTYPE html> declaration, which tells the web browser what kind of document it's dealing with. The main content is wrapped within <html> tags, which house two important sections: the <head> and the <body>.

The <head> section contains information that isn't directly displayed on the webpage, but is still important. It might include the page title, character encoding, and links to external stylesheets (CSS).

The <body> section is the heart of your webpage. This is where you'll place all the visible content, like headings, paragraphs, images, and links.

Essential HTML Tags:

Now that you have the basic structure, let's explore some fundamental tags to bring your webpage to life:

Headings (<h1> to <h6>): Use these tags to create headings of different sizes, with <h1> being the largest and <h6> the smallest. Headings help structure your content and improve readability.

Paragraphs (<p>): Define paragraphs of text using the <p> tag. This creates a clear separation between different sections of content.

Images (<img>): Display images on your webpage using the <img> tag. You'll need to specify the image source (location) within the tag.

Links (<a>): Create hyperlinks with the <a> tag. This allows users to navigate to other webpages or sections within your current page.

Building Your First Webpage:

Ready to put your newfound knowledge into action? Here's a simple example of a basic HTML document:

HTML

```
<!DOCTYPE html>
<html>
<head>
  <title>My First Webpage</title>
</head>
<body>
  <h1>Welcome to My Website!</h1>
  <p>This is my very first webpage. Isn't it exciting?</p>
  <img src="image.jpg" alt="My Website Image">
    <p>Click <a href="https://www.example.com">here</a> to
visit another website.</p>
</body>
</html>
```

Use code with caution.

Save this code as an .html file (e.g., index.html) and open it in your web browser.

1.1.1 The Basic Structure of an HTML Document

Every website you visit, from news platforms to online stores, is built using a specific language called HTML. Think of HTML as the blueprint for a house – it defines the overall structure and organization of the content. Just like a house needs a foundation, walls, and a roof, an HTML document has a specific format that ensures the web browser can interpret and display the content correctly.

Let's delve into the essential components of an HTML document:

The Declaration (<!DOCTYPE html>): This line acts as the introduction, informing the web browser that the document is written in HTML. It specifies the document type and helps the browser render the content accurately.

The Root Element (<html>): This tag acts as the container for the entire HTML document. Everything from the page title to the content itself is wrapped within the <html> tag and its closing tag </html>.

The Head (<head>): This section holds information that's crucial for the webpage but isn't directly displayed to the user. Think of it as the behind-the-scenes area. Here you might find:

The Title (<title>): This tag defines the title of your webpage, which appears in the browser tab and search engine results.

Character Encoding (<meta charset="UTF-8">): This specifies the character set used in your document, ensuring proper display of different languages and symbols.

Links to Stylesheets (<link>): This tag allows you to link external CSS files that define the visual styles of your webpage (covered later in the book).

The Body (<body>): This is the heart and soul of your webpage. Everything the user sees on the screen, from text and images to headings and links, resides within the <body> tags. This is where you'll use various HTML tags to structure and display your content.

Here's a simple illustration of this structure:

```
HTML
<!DOCTYPE html>
<html>
<head>
 <title>My Webpage</title>
</head>
<body>
```

```
<h1>Welcome!</h1>
<p>This is the content of my webpage.</p>
</body>
</html>
```
Use code with caution.

This basic structure provides a strong foundation for building any webpage. As you progress through your HTML learning journey, you'll explore a variety of tags within the <body> section to create more complex and engaging content. Remember, a well-structured HTML document is essential for both a user-friendly browsing experience and proper search engine optimization (SEO).

1.1.2 Essential HTML Tags and Elements

Now that you understand the basic structure of an HTML document, it's time to dive into the building blocks that bring your webpage to life: HTML tags and elements. These tags act like labels, instructing the web browser how to interpret and display the content you provide.

Headings (<h1> to <h6>):

Headings are crucial for structuring your content and improving readability. HTML offers a range of heading tags, from <h1> (largest) to <h6> (smallest). Use these tags to define the hierarchy of your content, with <h1> typically used for the main title of your page and subsequent headings for subsections.

Paragraphs (<p>):

The <p> tag is your go-to for defining paragraphs of text. It creates a clear separation between different sections of content and enhances the visual flow of your webpage. Remember to use separate <p> tags for each distinct paragraph.

Images (<img>):

Images add visual interest and can break up large chunks of text. The <img> tag allows you to embed images within your webpage. Here's what you'll need to specify within the tag:

src: This attribute defines the location (source) of the image file. Ensure the path is accurate relative to your HTML document.
alt: This attribute provides alternative text for the image, which is crucial for accessibility. The alt text is displayed if the image cannot be loaded or for users who rely on screen readers.
Links (<a>):

Hyperlinks, commonly known as links, are the cornerstone of web navigation. The <a> tag allows you to create links that, when clicked, take users to another webpage, a specific section within your current page, or even an external resource like an email address. Here's a breakdown of the key attributes:

href: This attribute specifies the destination URL of the link. Where should the user be directed upon clicking?
text: This defines the visible text that users will see and click on. Make your link text descriptive and informative.
Lists (<ul> for unordered, <ol> for ordered):

Lists help organize information into clear and concise sections. There are two main types of lists in HTML:

Unordered lists (<ul>): Use this for lists where the order of items doesn't necessarily matter, such as a grocery list or a collection of features. Each list item is denoted by the <li> tag.
Ordered lists (<ol>): This type is ideal for situations where the order is important, like steps in a recipe or a chronological timeline. Similar to unordered lists, each item is defined by the <li> tag.
These are just a few fundamental HTML tags that form the foundation of any webpage. As you explore further, you'll discover a wider range of tags for specific purposes, such as:

<strong> and <em> for emphasizing text (bold and italic)

<table> for creating tables

 for inserting line breaks

<a href="#here"> for creating links to specific sections within your webpage (anchor links)

By mastering these essential tags and elements, you'll be well on your way to building engaging and informative webpages. Remember, practice is key! Experiment with different combinations of tags to create the desired structure and visual appeal for your web creations.

1.1.3 Creating Headings and Paragraphs

Headings and paragraphs are the bread and butter of any well-structured webpage. They work together to organize your content, improve readability, and guide users through your information.

Headings: Setting the Stage

Headings act like headlines in a newspaper, instantly grabbing the reader's attention and conveying the main points of your content.

HTML offers a variety of heading tags, ranging from <h1> (largest and most important) to <h6> (smallest).

Here's how to effectively use headings:

Structure and Hierarchy: Think of headings as an outline for your webpage. Use <h1> for the main title of your page and then progressively smaller headings (<h2>, <h3>, etc.) for subsections within your content. This creates a clear hierarchy and guides users through the logical flow of information.

Descriptive and Concise: Keep your heading text clear and concise, accurately reflecting the content of the following section. Descriptive headings not only enhance user experience but also play a role in search engine optimization (SEO).

Visual Appeal: Headings typically have a larger font size and sometimes bolder text compared to paragraphs. This visual distinction helps users scan the page and quickly grasp the overall structure of your content.

Paragraphs: Building the Body

Paragraphs are the workhorses of your webpage, carrying the main body of your text content. They define distinct sections of information and improve readability by creating natural breaks between different ideas.

Here are some key points to remember when using paragraphs:

Logical Flow: Organize your paragraphs in a logical sequence, ensuring a smooth flow of information for the reader. Each paragraph should ideally focus on a single thought or idea.

Conciseness and White Space: While paragraphs provide structure, avoid excessively long blocks of text. Strive for concise paragraphs with adequate white space between them. This improves readability and prevents overwhelming the user with a dense wall of text.

Formatting Options (Optional): While basic HTML doesn't offer extensive paragraph formatting options, you can utilize Cascading Style Sheets (CSS) later on to control aspects like text alignment and indentation.

Example:

Here's a simple example demonstrating how headings and paragraphs work together:

HTML
<h1>Welcome to My Amazing Website!</h1>
<p>This is the first paragraph of my webpage. It provides a brief introduction to the content you'll find here. Keep your paragraphs concise and to the point, making it easier for users to read and digest the information.</p>

```
<h2>Let's Dive Deeper</h2>
<p>This is the second paragraph, falling under the subheading
"Let's Dive Deeper." It elaborates on the introductory
information, providing more details about the website's purpose
or content.</p>
```
Use code with caution.

By effectively using headings and paragraphs, you can create
webpages that are not only informative but also visually appealing
and user-friendly. Remember, clear and well-organized content
keeps users engaged and coming back for more.

1.1.4 Adding Images and Links

Text is essential for conveying information, but images and links
can take your webpage to the next level by adding visual interest,
interactivity, and further exploration opportunities.

Images: A Window to Visual Storytelling

Images can break up large blocks of text, enhance understanding, and add a touch of personality to your webpage. They can be used for various purposes, such as:

Product photos: In an online store, high-quality product images are crucial for showcasing your offerings.
Explanatory diagrams: Complex concepts can be clarified with the help of well-designed diagrams or illustrations.
Background images: A subtle background image can set the tone and mood of your webpage.

Here's how to add images using the <img> tag in HTML:

src: This attribute specifies the location (source) of the image file. Ensure the path is accurate relative to your HTML document.
alt: This attribute provides alternative text for the image, which is crucial for accessibility. The alt text is displayed if the image cannot be loaded or for users who rely on screen readers. Always include a descriptive alt text for your images.

Links: The Web of Navigation

Links are the interactive elements that power navigation on the web. They allow users to jump to different sections within your webpage, explore external websites, or even trigger actions like downloading a file or sending an email.

The <a> tag is your gateway to creating links. Here's a breakdown of the key attributes:

href: This attribute specifies the destination URL of the link. Where should the user be directed upon clicking?
Text: This defines the visible text that users will see and click on. Make your link text clear and descriptive, indicating where the link leads.

Adding Interactivity:

Links can also be used to create interactive elements within your webpage. For example, you can create:

* **Buttons:** Style a link with CSS to resemble a button, allowing users to trigger actions like submitting a form.
* **Navigation menus:** Create a series of linked items that users can click on to navigate different sections of your webpage.

Example:

Let's look at an example incorporating both images and links:

HTML
<h1>My Photography Portfolio</h1>
<img src="portfolio.jpg" alt="A portfolio showcasing various photographs">

```
<p>Welcome to my photography portfolio! Click on the images
to view them in a larger format.</p>

<a href="nature.html">Nature Photography</a> |
<a href="travel.html">Travel Photography</a>

<p>I specialize in capturing the beauty of nature and the essence
of travel experiences. Explore my galleries to see more!</p>
```
Use code with caution.

In this example, the image showcases the photographer's work, while the links provide easy navigation to specific galleries. Remember, effective use of images and links can significantly enhance the user experience of your webpage, making it more engaging and informative.

1.1.4 Adding Images and Links

Text is the foundation of any webpage, but it's images and links that truly elevate the user experience. Images add visual interest, break up text monotony, and can even convey information more effectively than words alone. Links, on the other hand, power navigation, allowing users to explore different sections of your website or venture out to the vast web beyond.

Images: The Power of Visual Storytelling

A well-placed image can be worth a thousand words. Images can be used for a variety of purposes on your webpage:

Showcase products or services: In an online store, high-quality product images are crucial for attracting customers.

Explain complex concepts: Diagrams, illustrations, and infographics can clarify intricate ideas and processes.
Set the mood and tone: A captivating background image can establish the overall atmosphere of your website.

Enhance emotional connection: Images can evoke emotions and create a lasting impression on visitors.
Remember, effective image usage goes beyond aesthetics. Here are some key points to consider:

Image quality: Use high-resolution images that appear crisp and clear on different screen sizes.
File size optimization: Large images can slow down loading times. Utilize tools to compress images without sacrificing quality.

Accessibility: Always include descriptive alt text for your images. This text is displayed if the image cannot be loaded and is crucial for visually impaired users who rely on screen readers.

Links: The Web of Exploration

Links are the interactive elements that empower users to navigate your website and explore the wider web. They allow you to:

Create navigation menus: Organize a series of linked items that users can click on to access different sections of your webpage.
Link to external resources: Provide links to relevant websites, articles, or documents to enhance the user experience and offer additional information.
Trigger actions: Links can be styled with CSS to resemble buttons, allowing users to perform actions like submitting a form or downloading a file.
Here's a breakdown of the essential attribute for creating links with the <a> tag:

href: This attribute specifies the destination URL of the link. Where should the user be directed upon clicking?
Link Best Practices:

Descriptive link text: Don't use generic text like "Click here." Indicate where the link leads to keep users informed of what to expect.

Consider opening links in new tabs: Use the target="_blank" attribute within the <a> tag to open linked webpages in a new browser tab. This ensures users don't lose their place on your current page.

Visual cues for links: While not required by HTML, using underlines or slightly different text color can help users identify links on your webpage.

Example:

Let's look at an example incorporating both images and links:

HTML
```
<h1>Delicious Recipes from Around the World</h1>
<img src="world_cuisine.jpg" alt="A collage of dishes from various cultures">


<p>Welcome to my recipe website! Explore a variety of culinary delights from different corners of the globe.</p>

<ul>
  <li><a href="italian_recipes.html">Italian Classics: Pasta, Pizza & More</a></li>
    <li><a href="asian_cuisine.html">Aromatic Adventures: Exploring Asian Flavors</a></li>
  <li><a href="mexican_dishes.html">Spicy Delights: The Art of Mexican Cooking</a></li>
</ul>
```

```
<p>Click on the links above to discover scrumptious recipes and
embark on a culinary journey!</p>
```
Use code with caution.

By strategically using images and links, you can create webpages
that are not only informative but also visually engaging and
user-friendly. Remember, effective use of these elements enhances
navigation, improves user experience, and ultimately keeps visitors
coming back for more.

Chapter 2

Mastering the Art of CSS

Cascading Style Sheets (CSS) is the secret weapon in your web
development arsenal. While HTML provides the structure and
content of your webpage, CSS breathes life into it with style,
layout, and visual flair. It's like the fashion designer for your
website, transforming a bare-bones structure into a visually
appealing and user-friendly experience.

The Power of CSS:

Visual Appeal: CSS allows you to control the look and feel of your
webpage. From fonts and colors to backgrounds and borders, you

have the power to create a cohesive visual identity that aligns with your website's purpose.

Improved Readability: By using CSS to control elements like text size, line spacing, and margins, you can enhance the readability of your content.

Layout and Positioning: CSS empowers you to define the layout of your webpage. You can arrange elements like text, images, and navigation menus in a visually pleasing and logical manner.
Responsiveness: In today's world of diverse devices and screen sizes, responsiveness is crucial. CSS allows you to create webpages that adapt and adjust their layout to ensure an optimal viewing experience on any device, from desktops to tablets and smartphones.

The Building Blocks of CSS:

Selectors: These act like identifiers, targeting specific elements on your webpage. You can target elements by their tag name (e.g., <h1>), class (e.g., .special-text), or ID (e.g., #unique-element).

Properties: These define the specific visual styles you want to apply to your targeted elements. Common properties include color, font-family, background-color, margin, and padding.

Values: These specify the actual values for the properties. For example, the color property might have a value of red, while the font-family property could be set to Arial.

Putting it all Together:

CSS code is typically written in a separate file with the .css extension. You can then link this file to your HTML document using the <link> tag in the <head> section. Here's a basic example:

HTML
```
<!DOCTYPE html>
<html>
<head>
  <title>My Stylish Webpage</title>
  <link rel="stylesheet" href="style.css"> </head>
<body>
  <h1>Welcome to my Website!</h1>
    <p>This is some text content. Notice how it appears more stylish now!</p>
</body>
</html>
```
Use code with caution.

In the corresponding .css file (style.css), you could define styles for the <h1> and <p> elements, making your text appear more visually appealing.

Beyond the Basics:

While the fundamentals of CSS are relatively straightforward, the possibilities are vast. As you explore further, you'll delve into:

Cascading: Understanding how styles are inherited and overridden is essential for writing efficient CSS.
Pseudo-classes and pseudo-elements: These allow you to target specific states of elements (e.g., hovering over a link) or add stylistic flourishes (e.g., adding a border around an image).
CSS Frameworks and Libraries: These pre-written libraries provide pre-defined styles and layouts, saving you time and effort.
The Art of CSS:

Mastering CSS is not just about memorizing properties and values; it's about developing an eye for design and understanding how visual elements work together to create a cohesive and user-friendly experience. With practice and exploration, you'll transform your webpages from basic layouts to stunning and interactive creations.

By venturing into the world of CSS, you unlock a powerful tool for transforming your web development journey. Get ready to unleash your creativity and bring your web visions to life!

2.1 Introduction to CSS

Have you ever built a website using HTML and felt it was missing something? Sure, the structure and content are there, but it lacks personality, visual appeal, and that certain user-friendly flair. This is where CSS comes in, acting as the missing puzzle piece in your web development journey.

CSS: The Stylist of the Web

Cascading Style Sheets (CSS) is like the fashion designer for your webpage. While HTML provides the foundation – the structure and content – CSS breathes life into it with style, layout, and visual pizzazz. Imagine transforming a plain white t-shirt into a statement piece with vibrant colors and a unique design. That's the power of CSS!

Why Embrace CSS?

Here are some compelling reasons to dive into the world of CSS:

Visual Appeal: Transform your webpage from basic to beautiful. Control fonts, colors, backgrounds, and more to create a visually stunning and engaging experience for users.

Enhanced Readability: CSS allows you to fine-tune the presentation of your text. Adjust font sizes, line spacing, and margins to ensure your content is clear, easy to read, and visually pleasing.

Strategic Layout: Organize your webpage elements in a logical and visually appealing manner. CSS empowers you to position text, images, and navigation menus to create an intuitive and user-friendly layout.

Responsive Design: In today's diverse device landscape, websites need to adapt. With CSS, you can design webpages that adjust their layout for optimal viewing on desktops, tablets, and smartphones.

Getting Started with CSS Basics

The world of CSS might seem vast, but don't worry! We'll break it down into manageable pieces. Here are the fundamental building blocks:

Selectors: These act like identifiers, targeting specific elements on your webpage. Imagine them as tiny arrows pointing to things you want to style. You can target elements by their tag name (e.g., <h1> for headings), class (e.g., .special-text for a specific group of text elements), or ID (e.g., #unique-element for a single element).

Properties: These define the specific visual styles you want to apply. Think of them as the instructions for your targeted elements. Common properties include color for text color, font-family for the type of font, background-color for the element's background, and margin and padding to control spacing around the element.

Values: These specify the actual settings for the properties. For instance, the color property might have a value of red, while the font-family property could be set to Arial.

Putting it all Together:

CSS code is typically written in a separate file with the .css extension. You can then link this file to your HTML document using the <link> tag in the <head> section. Here's a basic example:

```
HTML
<!DOCTYPE html>
<html>
<head>
 <title>My Stylish Webpage</title>
 <link rel="stylesheet" href="style.css">
</head>
<body>
 <h1>Welcome to my Website!</h1>
   <p>This is some text content. Notice how it appears more stylish now!</p>
</body>
</html>
```

Use code with caution.

In the corresponding .css file (style.css), you could define styles for the <h1> and <p> elements, making your text bigger and bolder, perhaps even changing its color.

Ready to Explore Further?

This is just a glimpse into the exciting world of CSS. As you progress, you'll delve deeper into:

Cascading: Understanding how styles are inherited and overridden is essential for writing efficient CSS.
Pseudo-classes and pseudo-elements: These allow you to target specific states of elements (e.g., hovering over a link) or add special effects (e.g., adding a subtle shadow around an image).
CSS Frameworks and Libraries: These pre-written libraries provide a collection of styles and layouts, saving you time and effort.

The Art of CSS

Remember, mastering CSS goes beyond memorizing properties and values. It's about developing an eye for design, understanding how visual elements work together, and creating a user experience that is both beautiful and functional. With dedication and exploration, you'll transform your webpages from basic to breathtaking!

2.2 Styling Text with CSS

Text is the backbone of any webpage, conveying information and engaging users. But plain, unstyled text can appear bland and lack personality. This is where CSS comes in, empowering you to transform your text from basic to beautiful. With CSS, you can wield a magic wand and style your text to enhance readability, establish visual hierarchy, and create a cohesive brand identity for your webpage.

Diving into the Toolbox: Essential Text Properties

CSS offers a treasure trove of properties specifically designed to style your text. Here are some of the most commonly used ones:

Font Family: This property allows you to define the typeface used for your text. Experiment with different fonts (e.g., serif fonts like Times New Roman for a classic look, or sans-serif fonts like Arial for a clean and modern aesthetic) to find the perfect match for your webpage's tone and content.

Font Size: Control the size of your text to ensure readability across different screen sizes. Headings typically use larger font sizes for prominence, while body text utilizes a comfortable size for extended reading.

Font Weight: This property affects the boldness of your text. Use bolder fonts (higher font weight values) for headings and emphasis, while lighter fonts are ideal for body text.

Color: Set the text color to match your webpage's overall design scheme. Black is a popular choice for body text due to its high contrast, but don't be afraid to experiment with colors that complement your brand or visual theme.

Text Decoration: Add underlines, overlines, or strikethrough effects to your text using this property. While sparingly used for emphasis or specific purposes, avoid excessive text decoration as it can hinder readability.

Line Height: This property controls the spacing between lines of text. Adjusting line height can improve readability, especially for large blocks of text.
Example in Action: Styling a Paragraph

Let's see how these properties work together to style a paragraph:

HTML

```html
<p>This is a paragraph of text. But wouldn't it be more visually appealing if we styled it?</p>
```
Use code with caution.

Here's the corresponding CSS:

```css
CSS
p {
    font-family: Arial, sans-serif;   /* Fallback font if Arial is unavailable */
 font-size: 16px;
 line-height: 1.5; /* 1.5 times the font size for better spacing */
  color: #333333; /* A dark gray for readability */
}
```
Use code with caution.

This code defines styles for all <p> elements on the webpage. The paragraph now appears in a clear and readable Arial font, with increased line spacing for better visual flow. The color is set to a dark gray for improved contrast against a white background.

Beyond the Basics: Creative Text Styling

As you explore further, you'll discover even more ways to style your text:

Text Shadow: Add a subtle shadow effect to create depth and dimension.

Text Transform: Capitalize, lowercase, or even transform text into uppercase.

Letter Spacing: Adjust the spacing between individual letters for artistic effects or specific design requirements.

Remember:

While creative text styling can enhance your webpage, avoid going overboard. Strive for a balance that prioritizes readability and user experience. The goal is to make your text visually appealing without sacrificing clarity and functionality.

By mastering text styling with CSS, you can elevate your webpages from ordinary to extraordinary. So, unleash your creativity, experiment with different properties, and transform your text into a captivating design element!

2.3 Working with Colors, Fonts, and Backgrounds

Cascading Style Sheets (CSS) empowers you to become the artist of your webpage, wielding color, fonts, and backgrounds to create a visually stunning and engaging user experience. These design elements work together to establish your webpage's personality, brand identity, and overall aesthetic.

The Power of Color

Colors evoke emotions, set the mood, and guide users through your webpage. Here's how to harness the power of color with CSS:

Choosing a Color Scheme: Select a primary and secondary color palette that complements each other and aligns with your brand or webpage's purpose. Many websites use color theory principles to create harmonious color combinations.

Background Colors: Set the background color for your webpage sections or the entire page. Solid colors create a clean and modern look, while textured backgrounds can add depth and visual interest.

Text Color: Ensure proper contrast between text color and background for optimal readability. Black text on a white background is a safe choice, but don't be afraid to experiment with colors within your chosen scheme.

Link Colors: Define the color of your links in their normal state and when hovered over by the user. This helps users identify clickable elements and provides visual feedback during interaction.

Finding the Perfect Font

The font you choose plays a crucial role in conveying the tone and personality of your webpage. Here are some key considerations:

Font Family: Select a font family that aligns with your webpage's purpose and target audience. Serif fonts (e.g., Times New Roman) exude a classic and professional feel, while sans-serif fonts (e.g., Arial) offer a clean and modern aesthetic.
Font Size: Establish a hierarchy of font sizes for headings, subheadings, body text, and captions. Headings should be larger for prominence, while body text should be comfortable for extended reading.

Font Weight: Control the boldness of your text. Use bolder fonts for emphasis or headings, and lighter fonts for regular text.
Setting the Stage: Backgrounds

Backgrounds can add visual interest, establish a mood, and even create a sense of depth on your webpage. Here's how to leverage backgrounds with CSS:

Background Color: As mentioned earlier, background colors can be set for specific sections or the entire webpage.

Background Images: Integrate images as website backgrounds. Choose high-resolution images that complement your design and don't overwhelm the content. Optimize image file sizes to avoid slow loading times.

Background Gradients: Create smooth color transitions using CSS gradients. This can add a subtle touch of dynamism to your webpage.

Putting it all Together:

Imagine a webpage with a clean white background, headings in a bold blue sans-serif font, and body text in a slightly lighter shade of blue. Links might be displayed in a contrasting orange color, changing to a slightly darker shade on hover. This is just a basic example, but it demonstrates how colors, fonts, and backgrounds work together to create a cohesive visual experience.

Beyond the Basics:

As you delve deeper into CSS, you'll explore:

Color Transparency: Control the opacity of colors, allowing you to create translucent elements or overlays.
Font Combinations: Experiment with combining different font families for headings and body text to create a unique style.

Background Positioning: Precisely position background images to create specific effects or highlight certain elements.

Remember:

Balance and Consistency: Strive for a balance between colors, fonts, and backgrounds to avoid overwhelming users. Maintain consistency throughout your webpage for a unified look and feel. Accessibility: Ensure color contrast meets accessibility standards, especially for users with visual impairments.

By mastering these design elements, you can transform your webpages into visually appealing and user-friendly masterpieces. So, unleash your inner artist, grab your CSS paintbrush, and start creating!

2.4 Applying Layouts with CSS

Cascading Style Sheets (CSS) goes beyond just making your webpage look pretty. It empowers you to act as the architect, structuring and arranging the various elements (text, images, navigation menus, etc.) to create a well-organized and user-friendly layout. An effective layout ensures a smooth user experience by guiding visitors through your content in a logical and intuitive way.

The Building Blocks of Layout with CSS

CSS offers a variety of tools to control the positioning and arrangement of elements on your webpage. Here are some of the fundamental concepts:

The Box Model: Imagine every element on your webpage as a box with content, padding, margin, and border. CSS allows you to manipulate these properties to control the element's overall size and placement.

Floats: While a historical layout method, floats are still relevant for specific situations. They allow elements to float to the left or right of their container, enabling basic multi-column layouts.

Positioning: CSS offers various positioning properties like static (default position in the document flow), relative (shifted relative to its normal position), absolute (positioned relative to its nearest positioned ancestor), and fixed (positioned relative to the viewport). These properties provide granular control over element placement.

Modern Layout Techniques:

With the advent of more sophisticated CSS features, we now have powerful layout techniques for creating complex and responsive webpages. Here are two key approaches:

Flexbox: This method treats elements like flexible containers that can be resized and distributed within the available space. It's ideal for creating single-dimensional layouts (rows or columns) with flexible sizing and alignment options.
CSS Grid: This powerful layout system allows you to define rows and columns, creating a grid-like structure. Elements can then be placed within these grid cells, enabling complex and responsive layouts with precise control over positioning and alignment.

Choosing the Right Layout Technique:

The best layout technique depends on the complexity of your webpage and your desired outcome.

Simple Layouts: Floats or basic positioning might suffice for simpler layouts with a few columns or sidebars.
Flexible Layouts: Flexbox is a great choice for layouts where elements need to resize and adapt to different screen sizes.
Complex Layouts: For intricate layouts with precise grid-like structures, CSS Grid offers the most control and flexibility.

Remember:

Responsiveness: In today's world of diverse devices, ensure your layout adapts and adjusts for optimal viewing on desktops, tablets, and smartphones. Use responsive design techniques in conjunction with CSS layouts.

Usability: The ultimate goal of your layout is to create a user-friendly experience. Strive for a clear hierarchy, logical flow, and easy navigation.

By mastering CSS layout techniques, you can transform your webpages from disorganized structures to intuitive and visually appealing experiences. So, grab your CSS toolbox and start architecting stunning and functional layouts!

Part 2: Building Modern Websites

Chapter 3

In today's digital landscape, where users access webpages from a multitude of devices – desktops, laptops, tablets, and smartphones – creating websites that adapt and adjust is no longer a luxury, it's a necessity. This is where responsive design comes in, and CSS plays a vital role in making it happen. Responsive design principles ensure your webpage delivers an optimal viewing experience regardless of the screen size.

Core Principles of Responsive Design:

Mobile-First Approach: A core principle is to design for the smallest screens first (mobiles) and then progressively enhance the layout for larger devices (tablets and desktops). This ensures a smooth user experience on the most widely used devices.

Fluid Grids: Ditch fixed-width layouts! Instead, utilize fluid grids that expand and contract based on the available screen size. Think of it like a flexible container that adjusts its dimensions to accommodate different devices.

Flexible Images and Media: Images and other media elements should also adapt to the screen size. Use CSS techniques like max-width and height: auto to ensure images resize proportionally

47

Media Queries: Media queries are like conditional statements in CSS. They allow you to define specific styles for different screen sizes or device orientations (portrait vs. landscape mode). For example, you might hide certain elements or change their layout on smaller screens to optimize space.

Benefits of Responsive Design:

Enhanced User Experience: Users on any device can access your webpage with ease, leading to increased satisfaction and engagement.

Improved SEO (Search Engine Optimization): Responsive design is a ranking factor for search engines like Google. A website that adapts well is more likely to be displayed prominently in search results.

Reduced Maintenance: Maintain a single website that adapts across devices, eliminating the need for separate mobile and desktop versions.

Implementing Responsive Design with CSS:

Here's a glimpse into how CSS helps achieve responsive design:

Responsive Grid Systems: CSS frameworks like Bootstrap or Foundation provide pre-built grid systems that are inherently responsive, making layout creation for multiple screens much faster and easier.

Media Queries: Embed media queries within your CSS code to target specific screen sizes or device orientations. Then, define styles that adjust the layout, font sizes, and other elements for optimal viewing on those devices.

Beyond the Basics:

As you delve deeper into responsive design, you'll explore:

Viewport Units: Units like vh (viewport height) and vw (viewport width) are crucial for creating truly responsive layouts that scale relative to the user's viewport size.

Breakpoints: These define the points at which your layout changes to adapt to different screen sizes. Choosing the right breakpoints is essential for a smooth transition across devices.

Responsive Images: Techniques like srcset and picture element allow you to specify different image versions for various screen resolutions, ensuring optimal image quality and loading times.

Remember:

Responsive design is an ongoing process. As new devices and screen sizes emerge, you might need to refine your media queries and layouts to maintain a seamless user experience. However, the effort invested reaps significant rewards in terms of user satisfaction, SEO benefits, and overall website maintainability.

By embracing responsive design principles and wielding the power of CSS, you can ensure your webpages are accessible, user-friendly, and visually appealing on any device, creating a truly future-proof online presence.

3.1 What is Responsive Design?

Responsive design is a web design approach that ensures your webpage looks and functions optimally across all devices, from desktops and laptops to tablets and smartphones. It's all about creating a flexible and adaptable website that adjusts its layout and elements based on the screen size a user is viewing it on.

Here's a breakdown of the key concepts:

Why is Responsive Design Important?

Mobile-First World: Nowadays, a significant portion of web browsing happens on mobile devices. Responsive design guarantees a positive experience for these users, keeping them engaged and coming back for more.

Search Engine Optimization (SEO): Search engines like Google favor websites that are mobile-friendly. Responsive design can improve your website's ranking in search results.

Reduced Maintenance: Maintaining a single responsive website is easier and more cost-effective than managing separate versions for desktops and mobiles.

Core Principles of Responsive Design:

Mobile-First Approach: As mentioned earlier, prioritize designing for mobile screens first. This ensures a solid foundation for the website's core functionality on the most widely used devices.

Fluid Layouts: Ditch fixed-width layouts! Responsive design relies on fluid grids and flexible elements that can resize and adapt to different screen sizes. Imagine a website layout that behaves like a flexible container, shrinking or expanding to fit the available space.

Flexible Images and Media: Images and other media elements should also be responsive. Use CSS techniques to ensure they resize proportionally and don't cause layout issues on smaller screens.

Media Queries: These are like conditional statements in CSS. They allow you to define specific styles for different screen sizes or device orientations (portrait vs. landscape mode). For instance, you might hide certain elements on smaller screens to avoid clutter.

Implementing Responsive Design with CSS

CSS plays a vital role in making responsive design a reality:

Responsive Grid Systems: CSS frameworks like Bootstrap and Foundation offer pre-built grid systems specifically designed to be responsive. These tools make creating layouts for multiple screens much faster and more efficient.

Media Queries: Embed media queries within your CSS code to target specific screen sizes or device orientations. Then, define styles that adjust the layout, font sizes, and other elements for optimal viewing on those devices.

The Benefits of Responsive Design

Enhanced User Experience: Users on any device can access and interact with your webpage with ease, leading to increased satisfaction and engagement.

Improved SEO: As mentioned before, responsive design is a ranking factor for search engines. A website that adapts well across devices is more likely to be displayed prominently in search results.

Reduced Maintenance: Maintain a single website that adapts across devices, eliminating the need for separate mobile and desktop versions.

In Conclusion

Responsive design is no longer a trend, it's a necessity in today's web development landscape. By embracing responsive design principles and leveraging the power of CSS, you can create websites that are accessible, user-friendly, and visually appealing on any device, ensuring a future-proof online presence.

3.2 Creating Responsive Layouts with Media Queries

The web has become a multi-screen world, with users accessing information from desktops, laptops, tablets, and smartphones. Responsive design ensures your webpage delivers an optimal experience regardless of the screen size. Media queries, a powerful feature of CSS, are your secret weapon for creating these flexible and adaptable layouts.

Understanding Media Queries

Imagine a media query as a question posed by your CSS code. The question is typically about the characteristics of the device being used to access the webpage. For example, a media query might ask: "Is the screen size smaller than 768 pixels wide?"

Based on the answer (yes or no), the media query applies specific styles defined within the curly braces {}. This allows you to tailor the layout, fonts, and other visual elements for different screen sizes, creating a website that adapts and adjusts for optimal viewing on any device.

Putting Media Queries into Action:

Here's a basic example:

```css
CSS
/* Default styles for all screens */
body {
  font-size: 16px; /* Default font size */
}


/* Styles for screens smaller than 768px wide */
@media only screen and (max-width: 768px) {
  body {
    font-size: 14px;  /* Smaller font size for better readability on smaller screens */
  }
}
```
Use code with caution.

In this example, the default font size is set to 16px for all screens. However, the media query targets screens with a maximum width of 768px (typical for tablets and smartphones). For these smaller screens, the media query applies a style that reduces the font size to 14px, enhancing readability.

Common Media Query Properties:

max-width: Target screens with a maximum width less than the specified value (ideal for smartphones and tablets).
min-width: Target screens with a minimum width greater than the specified value (ideal for larger tablets and desktops).
orientation: Target specific device orientations (portrait or landscape mode).

Beyond the Basics:

As you explore further, you'll delve into more advanced media query techniques:

Media Features Combinations: You can combine multiple media features within a single query using and or not operators for even more precise targeting.
Media Query Listeners: Leverage JavaScript to detect changes in screen size or device orientation and dynamically adjust styles based on those changes.

Tips for Effective Media Query Usage:

Start Mobile-First: Design your layout for mobile screens first, then progressively enhance it for larger devices.

Set Breakpoints: Identify key screen sizes where your layout needs to adjust and create media queries targeting those breakpoints.

Test Thoroughly: Test your website across various devices and screen sizes to ensure a seamless responsive experience.

Media queries, combined with your CSS mastery, empower you to create websites that transform and adapt to any screen. Embrace the power of responsive design and craft a web experience that is not only functional but looks fantastic on any device!

3.3 Building for Different Screen Sizes

The digital world is a mosaic of screens – desktops, laptops, tablets, and smartphones – each with unique viewing experiences. In this landscape, websites that cater to just one size are relics of the past. Building for different screen sizes is no longer optional, it's essential. This is where responsive design comes in, and CSS serves as your trusty toolkit for crafting adaptable layouts.

Responsive Design: The Core Principles

Responsive design ensures your webpage delivers an optimal viewing experience regardless of the device used to access it. Here's the foundation:

Mobile-First Approach: Prioritize designing for mobile screens first. Since a significant portion of web browsing happens on mobile devices, this ensures a solid foundation for user experience.

Fluid Layouts: Ditch fixed-width layouts! Responsive design relies on fluid grids and flexible elements that can resize and adapt to different screen sizes. Imagine a website layout that behaves like a flexible container, shrinking or expanding to fit the available space.

Flexible Images and Media: Images and other media elements should also be responsive. Use CSS techniques like max-width and height: auto to ensure they resize proportionally and don't cause layout issues on smaller screens.

The Art of Responsive Layouts with CSS

CSS plays a vital role in creating responsive layouts. Here are some key tools:

Media Queries: These are like conditional statements in CSS. They allow you to define specific styles for different screen sizes or device orientations (portrait vs. landscape mode). For instance, you might hide certain elements on smaller screens to avoid clutter.

Grid Systems: Many CSS frameworks like Bootstrap and Foundation offer pre-built grid systems specifically designed to be responsive. These grids provide a foundation for creating layouts that adapt to various screen sizes, saving you time and effort.

Beyond the Basics:

As you venture further into responsive design, you'll explore:

Breakpoints: These define the points at which your layout changes to adapt to different screen sizes. Choosing the right breakpoints is crucial for a smooth transition across devices. There are common breakpoints based on popular device screen sizes, but you can customize them based on your specific needs.

Viewport Units: Units like vh (viewport height) and vw (viewport width) are essential for creating truly responsive layouts that scale relative to the user's viewport size, ensuring proper scaling on any device.

Responsive Images: Techniques like srcset and picture element allow you to specify different image versions for various screen resolutions. This ensures optimal image quality and loading times, especially on devices with limited bandwidth.

Advantages of Building for Different Screen Sizes

Enhanced User Experience: Users on any device can access and interact with your webpage with ease, leading to increased satisfaction and engagement.

Improved SEO: Search engines like Google favor websites that are mobile-friendly. A responsive website is more likely to be displayed prominently in search results.

Reduced Maintenance: Maintain a single website that adapts across devices, eliminating the need for separate mobile and desktop versions.

Remember:

Responsive design is an ongoing process. As new devices and screen sizes emerge, you might need to refine your media queries and layouts to maintain a seamless user experience. However, the effort invested reaps significant rewards.

By embracing responsive design principles and wielding the power of CSS, you can build websites that conquer every screen, ensuring a future-proof online presence that caters to users on any device. So, unleash your creativity and craft websites that look fantastic and function flawlessly across the digital landscape!

Chapter 4
Adding Interactivity with JavaScript (Optional)

Cascading Style Sheets (CSS) excels at styling your webpage, making it visually appealing and organized. But what if you want your webpage to go beyond static content and respond to user actions? Here's where JavaScript (JS) comes in, acting as the spark that ignites interactivity and dynamism on your webpage.

JavaScript: The Language of Interaction

JavaScript is a versatile scripting language specifically designed to enhance webpages. It allows you to:

Respond to User Events: Capture user interactions like clicks, mouse movements, key presses, and form submissions. Imagine a button that changes color when hovered over, or a search bar that filters results as the user types.
Manipulate the DOM (Document Object Model): The DOM represents the structure of your webpage. JavaScript empowers you to dynamically add, remove, modify, and rearrange HTML elements, creating a more engaging user experience.
Control Multimedia: Add interactivity to audio, video, and animations using JavaScript. Imagine a video that pauses when the user clicks away from the webpage.

Interact with APIs (Application Programming Interfaces): JavaScript can communicate with external APIs to retrieve data or perform actions. This allows you to integrate features like weather updates, social media feeds, or interactive maps.

Examples of Interactive Elements with JavaScript

Here are a few examples of how JavaScript can add interactivity to your webpage:

Accordions: Clicking a heading expands or collapses its corresponding content.
Image Sliders: JavaScript can automate the rotation of images on your webpage.

Interactive Forms: Implement real-time validation as users fill out forms, ensuring they enter the correct data format.

Dynamic Menus: Create menus that adapt and adjust based on user actions or hover effects.
Learning JavaScript: Getting Started

The world of JavaScript might seem vast, but don't worry! Here are some initial steps to get you going:

JavaScript Code Placement: JavaScript code can be placed within <script> tags in your HTML file, or you can link to separate .js files for better organization.

Basic Syntax: JavaScript has its own syntax, but it shares some similarities with other programming languages. Learn about variables, data types, operators, conditional statements (if/else), and loops (for/while).

Event Listeners: These are functions that wait for specific events to occur (like a button click) and then execute the corresponding JavaScript code.

Beyond the Basics

As you progress, you'll delve deeper into:

DOM Manipulation: Explore methods to add, remove, modify, and interact with HTML elements using JavaScript.

JavaScript Libraries and Frameworks: Many pre-written libraries and frameworks like jQuery offer functionalities and shortcuts to simplify common JavaScript tasks.

The Power of Interactive Webpages

By incorporating JavaScript, you can transform your webpage from a static brochure into an engaging and dynamic experience. Users can interact with your content, receive feedback, and feel more immersed in your webpage.

Remember:

Balance is Key: While interactivity is great, avoid overwhelming users with too much movement or complex animations.

Accessibility: Ensure your interactive elements are accessible to users with disabilities, following WCAG (Web Content Accessibility Guidelines).

Unleashing Interactivity with JavaScript

JavaScript empowers you to breathe life into your webpages. With its ability to respond to user actions and manipulate the webpage's content, JavaScript is a valuable tool for creating a more engaging and interactive web experience. So, start exploring the world of JavaScript and discover the magic of interactivity!

4.1 Introduction to JavaScript (Basic Concepts)

The web has come a long way from static text and images. Today's websites are interactive, dynamic, and engaging, thanks in large part to a powerful scripting language called JavaScript (JS). Even if you're a complete beginner, understanding the basic concepts of JavaScript will open doors to creating a more dynamic and interactive web presence.

JavaScript: The Superstar of Interactivity

Imagine a webpage that reacts to your clicks, a form that validates your input as you type, or an image carousel that smoothly transitions between pictures. These are just a few examples of what JavaScript can achieve. It's the language that adds life and responsiveness to webpages, making them more user-friendly and engaging.

Building Blocks of JavaScript:

Variables: Think of variables as containers that hold information you can use throughout your code. You can give them names and assign values like numbers, text, or even more complex data.

Data Types: Just like in the real world, data comes in different forms. JavaScript understands different data types like numbers (integers or decimals), strings (text), booleans (true or false), and more.

Operators: Operators perform actions on your data. JavaScript provides mathematical operators (+, -, *, /), comparison operators (==, !=, <, >), and logical operators (&&, ||, !).

Control Flow: Your code doesn't always run straight through. Control flow statements like if/else and loops (for, while) allow you to make decisions and repeat actions based on certain conditions.

Functions: Imagine reusable blocks of code that perform specific tasks. Functions take inputs (parameters), execute their instructions, and can optionally produce outputs (return values). Putting the Pieces Together: A Simple Example

Here's a basic example to illustrate these concepts:

JavaScript

```
// Declare a variable to store a name
let userName = "Alice";

// Display a greeting using the userName variable
alert("Welcome, " + userName + "!");

// Check if the user's age is greater than 18
let userAge = 25;
if (userAge > 18) {
  alert("You are eligible to access this content.");
}
```

Use code with caution.

In this example, we define a variable userName to store a name, then use it to display a personalized greeting. We also check the user's age using an if statement and display a message accordingly.

Learning Resources to Kickstart Your Journey

The world of JavaScript is vast, but there's a wealth of resources available to help you get started:

Online Tutorials: Many websites offer interactive tutorials that guide you through the basics of JavaScript in a step-by-step manner.

Interactive Coding Platforms: Platforms like Codecademy or freeCodeCamp provide a fun and engaging way to learn JavaScript through coding challenges and exercises.
Books and Documentation: Classic books like "Eloquent JavaScript" or the official JavaScript documentation serve as excellent references as you progress.

The Benefits of Learning JavaScript

By understanding JavaScript even at a basic level, you can:

Enhance User Experience: Add interactivity and responsiveness to your webpages, making them more engaging for users.
Validate Forms: Ensure users enter data in the correct format before submitting forms.
Create Animations and Dynamic Effects: Bring your webpage to life with subtle animations or interactive elements.
Embrace the Challenge: A Rewarding Journey

Learning JavaScript might seem daunting at first, but with dedication and the right resources, you can unlock its potential. As you delve deeper, you'll discover a world of possibilities for creating dynamic and interactive web experiences. So, take the first step, start exploring, and unleash the power of JavaScript in your web projects!

4.2 Creating Simple Interactions with JavaScript

The magic of JavaScript lies in its ability to respond to user actions. Event listeners are like tiny sentinels waiting for specific events to occur on your webpage. When an event happens (like a button click or mouse hover), the corresponding JavaScript code springs into action.

Here are some common user events and their applications:

Click Events: Make a button change color when clicked, submit a form, or trigger an animation.
Mouseover/Mouseout Events: Swap images when the user hovers over them, or display hidden information on hover.
Keypress Events: Detect when a key is pressed, like enabling a search function when the user presses Enter.

Adding Event Listeners to Your Code

There are two main ways to attach event listeners to HTML elements:

Inline Event Handlers: This approach directly places JavaScript code within the HTML element using the onclick or onmouseover attributes. While convenient for simple interactions, it can make your code less organized for complex functionalities.

HTML

```
<button onclick="alert('Button Clicked!')">Click Me</button>
```

Use code with caution.

JavaScript Event Listeners: This method involves using JavaScript code to attach event listeners to elements after the HTML structure has loaded. It offers more flexibility and separation of concerns.

HTML

```
<button id="myButton">Click Me</button>
```

```
<script>
  // Get a reference to the button element
  const button = document.getElementById("myButton");

  // Add a click event listener to the button
  button.addEventListener("click", function() {
    alert("Button Clicked!");
```

```
});
</script>
```
Use code with caution.

Beyond the Click: Common Use Cases for Simple Interactions

Let's explore some creative ways to use JavaScript for basic interactions:

Image Gallery: Create a simple image gallery where users can click on thumbnails to display larger versions of the images.

Interactive Forms: Implement real-time validation as users fill out forms, ensuring they enter data in the correct format (e.g., checking for valid email addresses).

Accordions: Develop collapsible sections of content that expand or collapse when the user clicks on a heading.

Dynamic Menus: Create menus that change appearance or reveal sub-menus based on user hover interactions.
Tips for Effective Interactive Elements

Clarity and Simplicity: Focus on creating clear and intuitive interactions that enhance the user experience.

User Feedback: Provide visual or auditory feedback to users when they interact with elements (e.g., changing button color on click). Accessibility: Ensure your interactive elements are accessible to users with disabilities, following WCAG (Web Content Accessibility Guidelines).
Remember:

These are just the building blocks! As you explore further, you'll delve into:

DOM Manipulation: Learn how to dynamically add, remove, modify, and interact with HTML elements using JavaScript.
JavaScript Libraries: Many pre-written libraries like jQuery offer functionalities and shortcuts to simplify common JavaScript tasks.

With a little practice and these foundational concepts, you'll be well on your way to crafting engaging and interactive web experiences using JavaScript. So, unleash your creativity and start adding a touch of magic to your webpages!

4.3 (Optional) Integrating JavaScript with HTML & CSS

Cascading Style Sheets (CSS) breathes life into your webpage with stunning visuals and layout, while HTML provides the core structure and content. But to create truly dynamic and interactive experiences, you need the third member of the dream team: JavaScript (JS). Here's how these three web development languages work together to create magic.

The Big Picture: Understanding the Roles

HTML (HyperText Markup Language): Imagine HTML as the skeleton of your webpage. It defines the structure and content elements like headings, paragraphs, images, buttons, and forms.

CSS (Cascading Style Sheets): Think of CSS as the artist's palette. It controls the presentation of your webpage, including fonts, colors, backgrounds, and layout. CSS uses selectors to target specific HTML elements and define their visual styles.

JavaScript (JS): JavaScript is the spark that brings interactivity to the mix. It responds to user actions (clicks, hovers, form submissions), dynamically modifies the content (HTML) and presentation (CSS) of your webpage, creating a more engaging user experience.

How They Work Together: A Collaborative Effort

The Foundation: HTML Structure: You start by building the basic structure of your webpage using HTML elements. Imagine a webpage with a button and a paragraph.

HTML
```
<button id="myButton">Click Me</button>
<p id="myParagraph">This paragraph will change!</p>
```

Use code with caution.

Adding Style with CSS: CSS takes the HTML structure and defines how it should look. You can style the button and paragraph using CSS selectors.

CSS
```
#myButton {
  background-color: blue;
  color: white;
  padding: 10px;
}

#myParagraph {
  font-size: 16px;
}
```
Use code with caution.

JavaScript Makes it Interactive: Now, JavaScript comes in to add interactivity. You can write code that listens for a click on the button and then modifies the content of the paragraph using the ID selector.

HTML

```
<script>
  // Get a reference to the button element
  const button = document.getElementById("myButton");

  // Add a click event listener to the button
  button.addEventListener("click", function() {
    const paragraph = document.getElementById("myParagraph");
    paragraph.textContent = "The paragraph has changed!";
  });
</script>
```

Use code with caution.

Benefits of Integration: A Powerful Trio

By combining HTML, CSS, and JavaScript, you achieve:

Structured and Dynamic Webpages: HTML provides the foundation, CSS styles the presentation, and JavaScript injects interactivity, creating a well-rounded webpage.

Enhanced User Experience: Interactive elements like clickable buttons, dynamic content updates, and form validation lead to a more engaging experience for users.

Clear Separation of Concerns: Each language plays a specific role, making your code more maintainable and easier to understand.

Examples of Integration in Action

Here are some everyday examples of how HTML, CSS, and JavaScript work together:

Interactive Forms: The form is built with HTML, styled with CSS, and JavaScript might handle real-time validation and error messages.

Image Sliders: HTML structures the slider, CSS defines its appearance, and JavaScript automates image transitions or user interaction with the slider.

Accordions: HTML creates the accordion elements, CSS styles them, and JavaScript controls the expand/collapse functionality based on user clicks.

Remember:

Planning is Key: Before diving in, plan the structure, styles, and desired interactions for your webpage.

Start Simple: Begin with basic interactions and gradually build upon your knowledge.

Test Thoroughly: Ensure your integrated webpage functions as expected across different browsers.

By harnessing the power of HTML, CSS, and JavaScript together, you can transform static webpages into dynamic and interactive masterpieces. So, start collaborating with this dream team and bring your web creations to life!

Part 3: User Experience and Best Practices

Chapter 5
Designing for Usability

In to day's digital landscape, users have high expectations. Websites and applications need to be not only visually appealing but also intuitive and easy to use. This is where usability comes in. It's the foundation for creating user-centered designs that prioritize ease of use and user satisfaction.

What is Usability?

Usability is a measure of how effective, efficient, and satisfactory a user interface (UI) is for a specific user in a specific context. Here's a breakdown of the key aspects:

Effective: Can users achieve their goals with your product (website, app)? Is the functionality clear and easy to understand?
Efficient: Can users complete tasks quickly and without unnecessary steps? Is the interface streamlined and minimizes cognitive load?

Satisfactory: Is the user experience enjoyable and frustration-free? Does the design create a positive user perception?

Why is Usability Important?

Usability is not just a feel-good principle; it has real-world benefits:

Increased User Engagement: Usable interfaces keep users engaged and coming back for more.

Improved Conversion Rates: If users can easily find what they need and complete tasks, conversion rates (e.g., purchases, sign-ups) increase.

Reduced Support Costs: Usable interfaces require less user support as users can navigate and solve problems independently.
Enhanced Brand Reputation: A positive user experience builds trust and loyalty, leading to a stronger brand reputation.

Principles of User-Centered Design

Usability is achieved through a user-centered design approach. Here are some core principles:

User Research: Understand your target audience and their needs through user research methods like surveys, interviews, and usability testing.

Intuitive Interface: The design should be self-explanatory and follow established conventions. Users shouldn't have to guess how to interact with elements.

Clear Navigation: Make it easy for users to find what they're looking for with a clear and consistent navigation system.
Accessibility: Ensure your design is accessible to users with disabilities, following WCAG (Web Content Accessibility Guidelines).

User Feedback: Incorporate feedback mechanisms like surveys or contact forms to gather user input and iterate on your design.
Enhancing Usability with Visual Design

Visual design plays a crucial role in usability:

Visual Hierarchy: Use visual cues like size, color, and contrast to guide users' attention towards important elements.
Meaningful Visuals: Use icons, images, and graphics that are clear and relevant to the content.
Readability: Ensure good contrast between text and background colors, and choose appropriate fonts that are easy to read on all devices.

Beyond the Basics

As you delve deeper into usability, you'll explore:

User Interface (UI) Patterns: Learn about established UI patterns like search bars, shopping carts, and drop-down menus that users are familiar with.

Usability Testing: Conduct usability testing with real users to identify pain points and refine your design iteratively.

Accessibility Best Practices: Stay up-to-date on accessibility guidelines and best practices to ensure your design is inclusive.

Remember:

Usability is an ongoing process. As your user base grows and technology evolves, you'll need to continuously evaluate and refine your design to maintain a positive user experience.

By prioritizing usability, you can create user interfaces that are not only beautiful but also functional and enjoyable. This will lead to a successful product that users love to use!

5.1 Principles of User-Friendly Design

In the digital world, first impressions are everything. When it comes to websites and applications, users form an opinion within seconds of landing on a page. This is where user-friendly design principles come into play. These principles act as a guide to create interfaces that are not only aesthetically pleasing but also intuitive, efficient, and ultimately lead to a positive user experience.

The Pillars of User-Friendly Design

User-Centered Approach: This core principle emphasizes designing with the user in mind. It involves understanding your target audience, their needs, and their goals when interacting with your product. User research through surveys, interviews, and usability testing is crucial in this phase.

Intuitive Interface: Imagine an interface that feels natural to use, like riding a bike. Users shouldn't have to spend time figuring out how to interact with elements or complete tasks. Strive for a design that follows established conventions and is self-explanatory.

Clear Navigation: Getting lost in a maze of menus and links is a frustrating experience. A user-friendly design features clear and consistent navigation that allows users to find what they're looking for effortlessly. This includes a well-organized menu structure, breadcrumbs for context, and easily identifiable calls to action (CTAs).

Accessibility: An often overlooked but crucial aspect of user-friendly design is accessibility. Ensure your interface can be used by everyone, regardless of ability. Following WCAG (Web Content Accessibility Guidelines) is essential for creating inclusive designs that cater to users with disabilities, including visual impairments, motor limitations, and cognitive differences.

Minimalist Design: While visual appeal is important, avoid overwhelming users with clutter. Embrace the concept of "less is more." Focus on presenting only the essential elements and functionalities that users need to achieve their goals. Whitespace (empty space) plays a vital role in creating a clean and uncluttered user interface.

Seamless Interaction: User interactions with the interface should feel smooth and responsive. Provide clear feedback mechanisms, like progress bars or confirmation messages, to keep users informed about the outcome of their actions. Animations and transitions, if used, should be subtle and enhance the user experience, not hinder it.

The Power of Visual Design in Usability

Visual design plays a critical role in user-friendly interfaces:

Visual Hierarchy: Guide the user's eye towards important elements through visual cues like size, color, and contrast. Headings, buttons, and other crucial elements should be visually distinct to ensure users can prioritize their actions.

Meaningful Visuals: Images, icons, and graphics should be clear, relevant to the content, and enhance understanding. Avoid using stock photos that feel generic or inauthentic to your brand.

Readability: High-contrast text on a clean background is essential. Choose appropriate fonts that are easy to read on all devices, and consider font sizes suitable for different screen resolutions.

Beyond the Basics

As you venture into the world of user-friendly design, you'll explore:

User Interface (UI) Patterns: Leverage established UI patterns like search bars, shopping carts, and drop-down menus that users are familiar with. These patterns create a sense of comfort and predictability, reducing the learning curve for users.

Usability Testing: The best way to identify usability issues is to observe real users interacting with your design. Conduct usability testing sessions and gather feedback to iterate and refine your interface for optimal user experience.

Analytics and User Feedback: Don't just guess what users need. Utilize website analytics tools and user feedback mechanisms like surveys and contact forms to gather data and understand user behavior. This data can be invaluable in identifying areas for improvement.

Remember:

User-friendly design is an ongoing process. As technology evolves and user expectations change, you'll need to continuously evaluate and refine your interface. By prioritizing these principles and staying user-focused, you can create interfaces that are not just usable but also a joy to interact with. This will lead to a successful product that users will appreciate and keep coming back to.

5.2 Making Your Website Accessible

In the vast digital landscape, the internet should be accessible to everyone, regardless of ability. This is where website accessibility comes in. It's about creating websites that are usable and inclusive for people with disabilities. By following accessibility best practices, you can ensure a wider audience can perceive, understand, navigate, and interact with your website.

The Benefits of an Accessible Website

Moral and Ethical Imperative: Everyone deserves equal access to information and opportunities online. An accessible website is the right thing to do.

Increased Audience Reach: By catering to users with disabilities, you tap into a broader audience, potentially increasing website traffic and user engagement.

Improved Search Engine Optimization (SEO): Search engines like Google prioritize websites that are accessible. Accessibility compliance can positively influence your search ranking.

Reduced Legal Risks: Accessibility laws and regulations are becoming increasingly common. A well-designed website can help mitigate legal risks associated with website accessibility.

The Four Principles of Web Accessibility

The Web Content Accessibility Guidelines (WCAG) set forth four main principles that underpin website accessibility:

Perceivable: Content must be presented in a way that users can perceive. This includes providing alternatives for non-text content (like images with alt text descriptions), ensuring adequate color contrast for visual impairments, and offering options for audio content to be presented in text format.

Operable: The user interface and navigation must be operable. This means using keyboard navigation for users who cannot use a mouse, ensuring clear labels for buttons and form elements, and providing enough time for users to read and interact with content.

Understandable: The website's content and user interface must be understandable. This involves using clear and concise language, avoiding jargon, and providing explanations for complex information.

Robust: Content should be robust and compatible with a wide range of assistive technologies. This includes ensuring your website works with screen readers, supports different browsers and devices, and remains functional with assistive technologies used by people with disabilities.

Making Your Website Accessible: Practical Tips

Here are some actionable steps you can take to improve your website's accessibility:

Alt Text for Images: Always provide clear and descriptive alt text for all images on your website. This helps users who rely on screen readers understand the content of the image.

Keyboard Navigation: Ensure your website can be fully navigated using just the keyboard. This is crucial for users who cannot use a mouse.

Color Contrast: Maintain a good color contrast ratio between text and background colors. This is essential for users with visual impairments. Tools like WebAIM's Color Contrast Checker can help you assess contrast ratios.

Clear Headings: Use clear and descriptive headings to structure your content. This helps users with screen readers understand the organization of your webpage.

Focus Indicators: Make it clear which element on the webpage has focus (when a user tabs through using the keyboard). This helps users stay oriented and navigate efficiently.

Text Alternatives for Non-Text Content: Provide captions and transcripts for videos, and consider offering downloadable audio transcripts for complex audio content.
Accessibility Resources for Further Learning

The web accessibility community offers a wealth of resources to help you on your journey:

Web Content Accessibility Guidelines (WCAG): https://www.w3.org/WAI/standards-guidelines/wcag/ - The international standard for web accessibility.

WebAIM: https://webaim.org/ - A nonprofit organization dedicated to web accessibility. They offer a wealth of information, tools, and courses.

W3C Accessibility Initiative: https://www.w3.org/WAI/ - Provides resources and guidance on implementing WCAG.

Remember:

Website accessibility is an ongoing process. As you build and update your website, consider accessibility from the beginning. By following best practices, using available resources, and testing your website with accessibility tools, you can create a website that is inclusive and welcoming to everyone.

Chapter 6
Best Practices for Web Development

In the ever-evolving world of web development, adhering to best practices is crucial for crafting high-quality, user-friendly, and successful websites. Here's a breakdown of some key best practices to consider throughout the development process:

Planning and Organization

Clearly Defined Project Goals: Before diving into code, establish a clear roadmap with specific goals and functionalities for the website. What problem are you solving? Who is the target audience?

Wireframing and Prototyping: Create low-fidelity wireframes or interactive prototypes to visualize the website's layout, user flow, and core functionalities. This helps identify potential issues early on.

Version Control: Implement a version control system like Git to track changes, collaborate efficiently, and revert to previous versions if necessary.

Coding and Development

Semantic HTML: Structure your website using semantic HTML elements that accurately reflect the meaning and content of each section. This improves accessibility and search engine optimization (SEO).

Cascading Style Sheets (CSS): Separate presentation from content using CSS. This promotes cleaner code, easier maintenance, and a more consistent visual style across the website.

Separation of Concerns: Organize your code into logical components like reusable functions and well-defined classes. This makes your code more modular, maintainable, and easier to understand.

Responsive Design: Ensure your website adapts seamlessly to different screen sizes and devices (desktops, tablets, mobiles). Responsive design provides an optimal viewing experience for all users.

JavaScript Best Practices: If incorporating JavaScript, follow best practices like writing clean and maintainable code, using meaningful variable and function names, and utilizing appropriate event listeners. Consider using JavaScript libraries or frameworks for common functionalities.

Testing and Deployment

Thorough Testing: Test your website across different browsers and devices to ensure consistent functionality and visual appearance. Conduct accessibility testing to identify and address any accessibility issues.

Code Validation: Use code validation tools to identify and fix errors or potential problems in your HTML, CSS, and JavaScript code.

Deployment and Optimization: Choose a reliable web hosting service and optimize your website for fast loading times. Consider image compression techniques, code minification, and caching mechanisms.

Additional Best Practices

Security: Prioritize website security by following best practices like user authentication, data encryption, and regular security updates.

Performance Optimization: Focus on website performance by optimizing images, minimizing HTTP requests, and utilizing caching mechanisms. A fast-loading website provides a better user experience.

SEO Optimization: Implement SEO best practices to improve your website's ranking in search engine results pages (SERPs). This includes keyword research, meta descriptions, and website structure.

User Experience (UX) Design: Prioritize user experience by creating clear navigation, intuitive interactions, and a visually appealing design.

Staying Up-to-Date

The web development landscape is constantly evolving. Stay updated with the latest trends, best practices, and new technologies by following industry publications, attending conferences, and participating in online communities.

Remember: Following these best practices will guide you in creating robust, user-friendly, and successful websites that meet the needs of your target audience and thrive in the competitive online world.

6.1 Code Organization and Maintainability

In the realm of web development, where lines of code can sprawl like a tangled web, code organization and maintainability become the shining armor for developers. Just like a well-organized toolbox allows you to find the right tool quickly, well-structured code makes working with and modifying it a breeze.

Why is Code Organization and Maintainability Important?

Readability: Clean and organized code is easier to understand, not just for you but also for other developers who might collaborate on the project or inherit it later. Clear code structure and meaningful variable/function names make it self-documenting, reducing the need for extensive external documentation.

Maintainability: As websites evolve and new features are added, well-organized code is easier to modify and update. You can pinpoint specific sections for changes without getting lost in a maze of tangled logic.

Debugging Efficiency: Imagine encountering a bug in a complex codebase. A well-organized structure makes debugging significantly faster. You can isolate the problematic area and fix it efficiently.

Reduced Errors: Clear separation of concerns and modularity inherent in good organization practices can help prevent errors in the first place.

Key Principles for Organized and Maintainable Code

Modularization: Break down your code into smaller, reusable modules or functions. This promotes code reuse, reduces redundancy, and makes complex functionalities easier to manage.
Meaningful Names: Give your variables and functions descriptive names that clearly reflect their purpose. This enhances code readability and makes it easier for anyone to understand what each code block does.

Proper Indentation and Formatting: Consistent indentation and formatting improve code readability. It visually defines code blocks, loops, and conditional statements, making the code structure clear at a glance.

Commenting: While clean code should be self-documenting to a large extent, comments can be crucial for explaining complex logic or non-obvious sections of code. Use comments sparingly but effectively to provide clarity when needed.

Maintaining Organization as Your Codebase Grows

As your project progresses and the codebase expands, here are some tips to maintain organization:

File Structure: Organize your code files logically, grouping related functionalities together. Consider using a Model-View-Controller (MVC) or similar architecture to separate concerns.
Version Control: Utilize version control systems like Git to track changes, revert to previous versions if necessary, and collaborate efficiently with other developers.

Tools to Aid in Organization

Several tools can assist you in keeping your code organized:

Linters and Code Formatters: These tools automatically identify and flag potential coding errors and enforce consistent formatting styles.

IDEs (Integrated Development Environments): Many IDEs offer features like code completion, syntax highlighting, and code refactoring tools to improve organization and maintainability.

Remember:

Code organization and maintainability are not one-time efforts. They are ongoing practices that should be integrated throughout the development process. By prioritizing these principles, you'll be well on your way to crafting clean, efficient, and sustainable code that will serve you and your project well into the future.

6.2 Testing and Debugging Your Website

In the world of web development, launching a website isn't the finish line; it's the starting point for user interaction. But before you unleash your creation on the web, it's crucial to ensure it functions flawlessly. This is where testing and debugging come in – your trusty tools for identifying and fixing glitches, ensuring a smooth user experience.

The Importance of Testing and Debugging

Quality Assurance: Testing helps uncover bugs, errors, and inconsistencies in your website's functionality, visual presentation, and user experience. Fixing these issues before launch ensures a high-quality product that meets user expectations.

Improved User Experience: A well-tested website is a joy to use. By eliminating bugs and ensuring smooth navigation, you create a frustration-free experience for your users, keeping them engaged and coming back for more.

Enhanced Credibility: A polished and bug-free website reflects professionalism and builds trust with your visitors. It demonstrates attention to detail and a commitment to user satisfaction.

The Testing Arsenal: A Range of Techniques

Manual Testing: This involves manually navigating your website, clicking through links, filling out forms, and testing different functionalities from a user's perspective. It's a great way to identify usability issues and ensure the overall flow feels natural.

Automated Testing: Utilize automated testing tools to perform repetitive tasks and catch common errors. These tools can streamline the testing process and free up your time for more complex testing scenarios.

Cross-Browser Testing: Ensure your website displays and functions correctly across different web browsers (Chrome, Firefox, Safari, Edge, etc.) This is crucial as users access websites from a variety of browsers and devices.

Mobile Responsiveness Testing: In today's mobile-first world, it's essential to test your website's responsiveness on various screen sizes and devices (phones, tablets). A responsive design adapts seamlessly to different viewports, providing an optimal viewing experience for all users.

Accessibility Testing: Test your website's accessibility using assistive technologies and following WCAG (Web Content Accessibility Guidelines) to ensure everyone, regardless of ability, can access and interact with your website.

Debugging: The Art of the Fix

Identifying the Issue: Once you encounter a bug or error, pinpoint the root cause. Analyze error messages, retrace user steps, and use debugging tools to isolate the problematic area in your code.
Code Review: Carefully examine the relevant code section. Look for syntax errors, logical mistakes, or conflicts with other code elements.

Troubleshooting Techniques: Employ debugging techniques like using console logs to track variable values, setting breakpoints to pause code execution at specific points, and utilizing the debugger built into your browser's developer tools.

Resolving the Issue: Once you understand the cause, implement a fix by modifying the code. Test your changes thoroughly to ensure they resolve the issue without introducing new problems.
Tools for Effective Debugging

Browser Developer Tools: Your browser's built-in developer tools are your debugging companions. They provide features like error messages, console logs, a debugger, and the ability to inspect and modify HTML and CSS elements on the fly.

Code Linters and Static Analysis Tools: These tools can automatically identify potential coding errors and stylistic inconsistencies in your code, helping you catch issues early on in the development process.

Remember:

Testing and debugging are iterative processes. As you make changes and add features, retesting is essential. By incorporating these practices into your development workflow, you'll build confidence in your website's functionality and deliver a polished and user-friendly experience for your visitors.

6.3 Deployment and Going Live

In the web development journey, deployment and going live mark a pivotal moment. It's when your meticulously crafted website transitions from controlled development to the real world, ready to be experienced by users. This phase requires careful planning, execution, and a touch of vigilance to ensure a smooth launch.

Preparation is Key: Pre-Deployment Considerations

Before hitting the launch button, here are some crucial steps to ensure a successful deployment:

Thorough Testing: Exhaustive testing is paramount. Conduct manual testing, leverage automated testing tools, test across different browsers and devices, and ensure accessibility compliance. Fix any bugs or glitches that emerge during testing.
Code Optimization: Optimize your website's code for performance. Minify HTML, CSS, and JavaScript files to reduce file sizes. Optimize images for faster loading times. Consider caching mechanisms to improve website responsiveness.

Content Staging and Review: Prepare all the website content, including text, images, videos, and other multimedia elements. Ensure the content is accurate, up-to-date, and visually appealing. Stage the content in a staging environment, a replica of the live website, for final review and approval before deployment.

Deployment Environment and Hosting: Choose a reliable web hosting service that meets your website's needs in terms of bandwidth, storage, security, and scalability. Configure your deployment environment, which is the server-side infrastructure that will host your website's files and databases.

Deployment Methods: Taking Your Website Live

There are several methods for deploying your website, each with its own advantages:

Manual Deployment (FTP): This traditional method involves manually uploading website files and databases to the hosting server using File Transfer Protocol (FTP).

While straightforward, it can be time-consuming and error-prone for complex websites.

Version Control and Automation: Leverage version control systems like Git to manage code changes. Integrate deployment tools that can automate the deployment process, pulling the latest code from your version control repository and pushing it to the live server. This streamlined approach promotes consistency and reduces manual errors.

Continuous Integration/Continuous Delivery (CI/CD): For larger projects, consider implementing a CI/CD pipeline. This automates the entire development and deployment process, including testing, code building, and deployment to the staging and live environments. CI/CD ensures frequent updates and minimizes the risk of introducing regressions (bugs) during deployment.

Going Live: The Moment of Truth

Once you've deployed your website, it's go-live time! Here are some steps to follow:

Final Checks: Perform final checks on the live website to ensure everything functions as expected. Verify content accuracy, broken links, and proper form submissions.

DNS Propagation: If you've changed your website's domain name or hosting provider, allow time for Domain Name System (DNS) propagation to complete. This can take up to 24 hours for global visibility.

Monitoring and Analytics: Set up website monitoring tools to track website uptime, performance metrics, and user behavior. Utilize analytics tools to understand user traffic patterns and identify areas for improvement.

Post-Deployment Activities: Maintaining Momentum

Your website's launch is just the beginning. Here's how to maintain a healthy website after deployment:

Regular Backups: Schedule regular backups of your website's files and databases. This ensures you have a recovery point in case of unforeseen issues.

Security Updates: Keep your website's software, themes, plugins, and content management system (CMS) up-to-date with the latest security patches to address vulnerabilities and prevent security breaches.

Performance Monitoring: Continuously monitor your website's performance and identify bottlenecks that slow down loading times. Address performance issues promptly to maintain a positive user experience.

Content Updates: Keep your website content fresh and relevant by adding new content regularly. This encourages repeat visitors and improves search engine ranking.

Additional Considerations

Rollout Strategy: For large or complex websites, consider a phased rollout strategy. This allows you to deploy the website to a limited audience first, gather feedback, and fix any issues before a full public launch.

Communication: If your website launch coincides with a marketing campaign or rebranding effort, ensure clear communication channels are in place to inform users about the new website and its features.

Note:

Deployment and going live are exciting milestones in web development. By following these best practices, you can ensure a smooth launch, minimize potential problems, and set your website on the path to success. Embrace a data-driven approach, monitor your website's performance, and continuously make improvements to keep your users engaged and coming back for more.

www.ingramcontent.com/pod-product-compliance
Lightning Source LLC
LaVergne TN
LVHW051710050326
832903LV00032B/4125